Sweetheart of Special Education

By

Stacy Brannon

Table of Contents

Dedication iii

Acknowledgments iv

Introduction v

Chapter 1: Sincere 1

Chapter 2: Willing 9

Chapter 3: Eager 18

Chapter 4: Effortlessly 27

Chapter 5: Tactfulness 35

Chapter 6: Happy 44

Chapter 7: Empathetic 51

Chapter 8: Adaptable 57

Chapter 9: Realistic 64

Chapter 10: Timely 69

Conclusion 73

Dedication

This book is dedicated to the special education stakeholders across the world recognizing the abilities in students with disabilities.

Acknowledgments

I cannot take the full credit for the development of this book. I have had many guardian angels and supporters touch my life on my journey throughout special education. And you know who you are! Thank you sincerely from the bottom of my heart! Since this is my first published book, I would like to acknowledge my first special education teachers, my parents, Nancy and Ernest. Two amazing individuals who live by the principle of dedicated service to others through their purpose and passions. Thanks to my grandparents, who instilled the value of service to others. Jaylee, Jeremiah, and Jordan who will continue to find their area of service as they journey through life and identify areas of service for others. My extended family and friends who were there to encourage me or be a listening ear. My special education assistants who weathered through the years with me. And to the special education teachers across the world holding it down in your classrooms. I have major respect and love for you all!!! Thank you for all that you do to make a difference in the lives of students with abilities.

Introduction

In a world ruled by numbers, observational and statistical data, special education is no stranger to this routine practice. The three most touted words, "Document, Document, Document" has become the disclaimer for entering the world of special education. Don't worry; the next famous saying is as equally proclaimed, "If it wasn't documented, it didn't happen!" Sad, but unfortunately true as federal funding for special education relies on data and one receiving a paycheck. I know many of us did not enter this area of education for the money. Some of us entered because we were truly called. However, in the slowly evolving world of special education, the question remains, "If it has happened and it has been documented, why aren't we tackling the necessary issues that are being raised in the ominous world of special education?"

This book isn't written to address that, but it does cause one to wonder why parts of special education are slowly evolving in a world that is continuously changing. Does it not? Of course, we will be reminded there's a reason behind these changes. However, we never get to learn those reasons until the next school year when practices, policies, or a significant lawsuit happens to change the way we do our job duties (i.e., paperwork, identifying disabilities, and appropriate IEP verbiage).

This book is about rediscovering the purpose and passion behind all of us who continue to work in special education despite the atmosphere. I encourage you to read with an open mind and heart as everyone's journey is different but timely. The frustrations and concerns across the world felt by all stakeholders (i.e., educators, school leaders, parents, and students) inspired this book. There are legitimate concerns around the globe regarding the state of special education and its' service providers. But, we cannot continue to lose this battle due to lack of support, knowledge, understanding, and patience from one another to make the difference in these students' lives.

My name is Stacy Brannon. Nearly two decades of being a special education teacher, four degrees later, and teaching at every grade level in over four states; I have learned the art of mastering my journey in special education in each school year. I decided to give back to the profession successful strategies that I have implemented over the years. Hopefully, these strategies will impact your success in special education and your journey of serving students with disabilities.

"We only get one journey in this life. Choose your paths with purpose and passion, and wisely!"

Best Wishes,

Stacy Brannon.

DISCLAIMER: THERE WILL BE A MAJOR OCCURRENCE OF ACRONYM USAGE THROUGHOUT THIS BOOK. WELCOME TO THE WORLD OF SPECIAL EDUCATION!

Chapter 1: Sincere

I was never diagnosed with a disability. At least, that's the story my parents are holding on to. After teaching nearly two decades in special education, I can safely say that I have adopted ABCDEFGHIJKLMNOPQRSTUVWXYZ and its combination of acronyms. I certainly do not believe you need to have a disability to service people with disabilities. But, I do believe it does take a special person to teach special education! I never understood that statement until I matured in my role as a special educator. I started to notice that I was beginning to evolve in my own quirky special way after the 5th year of teaching special education. Warning: It's true!

I laughed it off as a joke when the veteran special education teachers tried to introduce me to their joys of teaching in the teacher's lounge during lunch times. They too seemed to be a little bit quirky. After teaching special education in four different states, I now have a greater understanding of how I adopted some of those characteristics. I also learned to stay out of the teacher's lounge after my first few years of teaching. It can sometimes be the TMZ show or the mental ward of the campus. Today, my lunches take place in my classroom or with trusted colleagues off campus. It's just my sincere attempt at maintaining my sanity in a pseudo-sane environment.

At the tender age of three, I had a sincere sense of discernment that led my heart to fight for the underdogs. It didn't matter what the person looked like, age, or ability level. It truly hurt my heart to see good people bullied or ostracized for circumstances outside of their control. While I do understand the concept of why hurt people hurt people, it's just not an acceptable behavior to me. My parents instilled early on that there's a way to fight those battles without coming across as a bully yourself. As special education teachers, we are the leaders in modifying and correcting inappropriate behaviors. Whether it be in our classrooms, dealing with difficult colleagues or parents, it is our ethical responsibility to raise awareness to the unmet needs of students with disabilities.

If you are called to this profession; you are not operating in the realm of fear. And you should be performing with a sense of sincerity. Special education teachers need to be ready to make strategic moves to improve practices within special education. The hemming and hawing of making necessary changes due to the threat of litigation or compliance issues are why we continue to remain stuck. Many of us special educators lose our credibility as professionals in the field when we are not taking appropriate actions. We cannot continue to not creatively think outside of the box due to fear or backlash. Those who are indeed called to this profession stand up for their helpless students and families. They face hard decisions with a sincere effort of righting injustices. They are not intimidated by others who throw around their power.

A sincere special educator sees and understands the bigger picture. Just because one has been in the district, at a school, or in a higher position longer does not indicate a sincere willingness to improve practices. People get stuck. Stuck in their mentality, their passions, and lose their sincerity. Having spent my entire career in this field, I have seen the good and the ugly in education leaders and colleagues. And also, the injustices in the system. There were times when I showed up to work frustrated, hurt, upset, lacked trust due to

3

these injustices. I knew those same injustices that I was feeling were the same injustices my students felt daily. Who was I to give up?

I am not perfect, nor do I claim to know the answers to many or even all of the issues affecting special education. I have made mistakes along the way. And I continue to make mistakes. The key is to learn and grow from those mistakes. We need to push aside our pride and competitive spirits to sincerely engage in supporting one another as colleagues and our students with disabilities. After all, we are the forgotten leaders on our school campuses. We dwell daily in the trenches (i.e., our classrooms) with students who require a sincere level of support. We set aside the pettiness of staff who have nothing better to do with their time than to criticize and prove what they know more about. No one cares how much you know. We care more about the action taking place behind what you know.

I admit I am guilty of labeling colleagues with diagnoses and secretly writing Individualized Education Plans (IEP) about them. I identify their areas of strengths and weaknesses. It's my way of dealing with my frustrations with colleagues who just don't get it. I do it with sincere intentions. Plus, it's an excellent therapy. It helps me to approach colleagues utilizing different goals and strategies to collaboratively be successful. I agree some colleagues can be difficult, but having a plan in place helps to work around their behaviors. Sincerity allows individuals to feel a level of trust and genuine support. Sincerity builds on transparent relationships which invites openness that allows for honest conversations. The first strategy of being sincere can be implemented using the following steps:

S - Surround yourself with positive and progressive-minded people, who are relentlessly making moves in special education. It is not enough to speak about changes but be a part of the changes. These amazing individuals will be your movers and shakers on your campuses. They keep the school in the know with resources, new initiatives, and ideas to improve special education practices. They recognize the demands but are not hindered by them. They will be flexible, understanding, but unwavering in their approach.

I - Imagine your students who show up to school daily to face their realities on a campus where they are deemed different and often made fun of. We are born with capabilities to help others. Think outside of your bubble and model this behavior for your students. Perhaps your students may have genius ideas that need sharing. Allow your imagination to build on your students' capabilities as well as your own.

N - Now is the time to share your gifts, talents, and solutions to resolve issues plaguing your special education departments. If you have a great idea, research it, and ask for a meeting to present it. Over the years, I would have "aha" moments, and I would request a meeting with the "who's who" over special education. You never know who may need to hear something at that time. If it does not happen, it is alright; at least you tried. Remember, it can happen in time just not in our time.

C - Calmly address areas in special education that you feel passionate about. At times, our passions can drive us to the point of no return. We need to remember that our desires may not always be received with the same excitement that we share. I have had to learn this the hard way. But I gained experience in researching, proposing and presenting ideas. It is a process, but it is achievable.

E - Elevate yourself in your role as a special education teacher by contributing more. Sometimes, this may be hard if you have obligations outside of school. Find creative ways that show you are serious about making a difference. Start a blog on providing resources to general education teachers and parents. Then the sky is your starting point, not the limit.

R - Right is right. It's just that simple. I was told in the sincerest way possible that I was not showing professionalism due to my timing issues. I tried to give every excuse in the book why I had not made it on time for a couple of meetings. But, deep down inside, I knew I wasn't sincere in my responses. I immediately wanted to point back the finger. Sometimes, we do have situations that occur outside of our control. If this happens, send a text or call to let the person know your status. I apologize for anyone's time that I had wasted. Another caveat to being right is to understand that you do not always have to prove you're right. Use this strategy based on the dynamics of your situation.

E - Equals in the profession, seeking to influence change in special education. Some of us are moved by things that affect us more than the other. But, do not discount anyone's sincere attempts to improve the state of special education with a hidden agenda. Trust me; you will run into people who will try to circumvent your efforts. They are ruled by limited thinking. Therefore, researching and doing your due diligence shows your sincere efforts to improve on areas of special education.

I began to realize over time that no one knows all there is to know about special education. I repeat this often throughout this book. Not even the experts, specialists, leaders, and researchers that we rely on. We look to our school leaders for support, but they are just as clueless as us at times. Every year, there are changes to laws or new school initiatives that affect how special education is delivered. When you think you have it down one year, there is a change for the next school year. Learning how to be willing to go along with the flow and still incorporate your personal yet sincere style is critical. Be sincere!

Chapter 2: Willing

In my first year as a teacher, I started off in general education. I taught 3rd grade in an inner-city school in Los Angeles, California. It was nestled in the heart of gang territory. I remember my family being worried about my safety. It was to the point that I was offered combat pay to teach at the school due to the high crimes in the area. But, I was willing to sign that contract. I knew I was called to be at this school for a reason. The way the cards lined up made it possible for me to even teach without a teaching credential. However, I was willing to work on obtaining my teaching credential once I signed my contract. This was back in the days before the many hoops to obtain a teacher's license was implemented. Thanks to good friends in good places, I started my journey into the realm of education without a license.

The school I taught at was year-round which afforded me the opportunity to substitute on my days off. During those months off, I chose to substitute different grade levels. I was willing to learn all there was about educating students. I used that opportunity to study classroom settings, décor, and teaching strategies. Yes, I did borrow not steal ideas, and I did ask for permission. I learned early on how teachers can interact with available materials. To this day, I still ask because I am still borrowing. During my classroom observations, I was also able to get a glimpse of the curriculum in which I knew I had to prepare my students for. It was a win-win situation.

There was one class I subbed for that became the game-changer for me in education. On the first day in class, I knew I was purposed for special education. It was an early intervention special education preschool class. I was tasked with working with 3 to 5 years old students with disabilities individually on an alphabet assignment. It was the letter C and crocodile was the lesson activity. I made a special connection with each one of those students individually. I remember the two Teacher Assistants (TA) in the classroom vividly as if it was yesterday staring at me in shock.

After the day was over, both TA's pulled me over to the side, and commented, "You were the first sub to get DJ to focus and finish his assignment. We have never seen him behave well with anyone besides our teacher!" And the other TA commented, "Will you be available to sub again? Our teacher is afraid to take off work because she knows subs don't understand her babies." At that moment, I knew I was purposed for special education. I felt universally aligned with my life's purpose the moment I sat down on the floor and ended the school day with circle time. Next, I knew I had to contact that teacher to find out what teaching credential I needed to obtain to teach this population of students.

However, the adventures of working in an inner-city school led to a lot of school lockdowns. I cringe every time I replay the gunshots in my head outside our classroom portable. I remember hiding under my desk while my 3rd graders were comforting me, and other students continued to work on their classwork at their desks. Helicopters and police sirens whirling around outside, but these students acted oblivious to the police showdown occurring outside the four walls of our classroom. I was embarrassed by myself and confused. I wondered why these students were not following the lockdown procedures I yelled out from underneath the desk. I felt like I was the student being schooled by 3rd graders.

The reason my students weren't affected is that this was everyday life for them. They learned early on how to survive in their environment despite the chaos ensuing around them. They were willing little individuals that taught me a great lesson in humility and pulled up my big girl panties.

It was a memorable lesson that will go down in my history book of teaching. After that, I willingly showed up to work every day regardless of external or internal influences. I knew I served a great group of students who depended on my strength and character to follow through despite my fears. Those of you 3rd graders in my first year of teaching, you are the reason I remain in education. You guys were the best group of students a first-year teacher could have asked for. I thank you for the many lessons you have taught me, and the laughter we shared. I pray that you all become contributing citizens to your community.

It was a couple of days later that I contacted the teacher I subbed for regarding her program. After learning all I needed to do, I immediately enrolled in a Masters' program in Special Education with an emphasis in Early Childhood Intervention. While working full-time, I attended classes at night for two years. It was a struggle, but due to my willingness to work with this age group, I endured the long working days and lecture-filled nights. One of the great experiences I had in the program was my opportunity to intern at Children's Hospital of Los Angeles alongside doctors, nurses, therapists, and patients. I was exposed to disabilities that I never knew existed. Whether I ever encountered these disabilities in the classrooms or not, I learned you never know which student with a disability will walk through your door. It was a learning experience and furthered my willingness to work with students with disabilities and their families even more.

It truly does take a special type of person to teach special education. They must possess certain qualities to ensure the job is being done correctly and appropriately. In Chapter One, we learned about the quality of being sincere. An individual must also possess a willingness to accept the tasks before them. Over the years, I have exuded a willingness in every position that I held within special education to perform the job to the best of my ability. I will share the following strategy I used to increase my willingness.

W - Work smarter at everything you do. I am guilty of not doing this at times. Sometimes, fatigue can set in after a hard, long day. But if you're willing to pick yourself up, get back on track, then you are in a willing realm. In this profession, one needs an organizational system that works for you. The key to surviving special education is staying organized. I am guilty of having my little-warped sense of organization. But, it works for me because I am willing to make an effort to improve on staying organized. Organizational systems can evolve over time. Do not worry if yours does not compare to others. Your organizational system allows you to keep track of your documents and meetings, and also affords you time. It assists in your willingness to get the job done.

I - Independently seek out opportunities to improve special education practices. Present at conferences, network with the community and include businesses sites as part of raising awareness to special education programs. The community can become your classroom. This is where transitioning can play a role in your lessons.

L - Lively dispositions help in situations that are changing. Yes, not everyone is going to have that lively, upbeat, positive, demeanor. But, you can choose to be that person who at least tries to or the person who feed into the negativity. Maintaining a lively disposition helps during times of change and chaos. Be willing to handle the punches that will come your way without having an adult tantrum. It also reminds others to relax and realize that situations will pass. Learn to stay put together and hopeful during chaotic situations.

L - Look beyond yourself for the answers as I have shared and will continue to share throughout this book. No one knows all there is about special education. I proudly include myself. We should become a free agent in raising special education awareness and sharing resources that will be useful to others. We should be able to tap into local, state, and international resources. The answers are available through other means.

I - Individualize goals that are set to fulfill your purpose for teaching special education. Identify key goals that will allow you to meet not only the needs of your student but for yourself as the professional. I guarantee you that your paths will cross with others on that same journey with similar goals. Together, you can build a strong team to conquer those goals. But, first, hone in on your individual goals and make them meaningful. Review them two to three times a week for confirmation.

N - Never forget your role in becoming a special education teacher. Our role is to provide educational services to students with disabilities. It is unfortunate but unavoidable; you will run into individuals who do not want your help. Just remember, some individuals live in a state of denial. But where there's a need, I believe we should at least try to find a way. Even if that means passing the individual to someone else who may be a better fit to help. Sometimes, there will be personality conflicts. But that doesn't mean the work doesn't need to be done. Be the solution, not the problem.

G - Give all that you can in your capacity. We can only do what we can do. As special education teachers, we want to provide the answers to the hard-hitting questions; however, we cannot possibly know all the answers. And it is okay! Allowing yourself to feel content in your role and your ability to carry out your role will increase your willingness to your all.

The beauty of willing to do increases eagerness to provide a quality education for students with disabilities. Eager people are not just sitting around dreaming about what could be done. Eager people are doers and go-getters. They are willing to seek change, improvement, and transformations.

This eagerness to become a special education teacher opened more doors for me in special education. Having a sense of eagerness within special education will take you many places. Special education needs sincere, willing, individuals who are eager. Will you be eager?

Chapter 3: Eager

After graduating from my Masters' program, I continued teaching at the same school in Los Angeles. I had done some job research and discovered a job fair being held in California for Hawaii. The state of Hawaii was experiencing shortages in the field of special education. They were eagerly searching different states for individuals interested in teaching in Hawaii. I knew it was a stretch, but I was eager to try it anyway. I signed up for the job fair and submitted the required materials. The interviews were held at a hotel near the Los Angeles airport (LAX). I remember walking in and seeing a line of people down the hallway. Immediately, I was overwhelmed and thought to myself what am I doing here? But, I didn't budge or think negative. I waited in the line just like everyone else had. I reviewed my resume and anxiously practiced my answers.

While waiting, I witnessed some faces that had been let down and other faces full of excitement as they exited the interview room. When it was my turn, I eagerly entered through the big mahogany doors into a room full of recruiters interviewing potential candidates. The buzzing of voices, nervous laughter and cough clearing throats adored the atmosphere. I took a deep breath. The lady who interviewed me was pleasant and had an inviting, bright smile. This helped to ease the pressure, but she dove right in with the necessary hard-hitting questions, instantly sending my heart down the elevator shaft to my stomach. Having only taught three years at that time in a tough neighborhood, I was able to relate my experiences to her questions in a creative way that even surprised me. Even she was shocked by my experiences in just three years of teaching. I was immediately offered the Early Childhood Intervention Special Education teacher position on the spot. I wanted to jump up, and dance like my excited students did whenever they got a question right in class. But instead, I moseyed on down the hall with a huge smile on my face passing other individuals eagerly waiting their turn. Let's say, the rest of the school year, I couldn't stop looking up at the airplanes that flew over the playground while monitoring kindergarteners at recess. I was eager to be on a plane with my family flying to Hawaii that summer. It gets better, folks.

Hawaii offered me a contract with a sign-on bonus for three years and paid for my moving expenses. I later learned that I would be opening a brand-new early intervention preschool unit. I was assigned to develop the program. It was the ideal set up. I was eager to get started. I would miss my students and my colleagues who I had become extremely close to. I learned a lot from the staff. I knew I could carry those experiences on to another campus. In those three years, I had taught all elementary grade levels and early childhood special education on the year-round model. The faculty presented me with an award for my three years of service and congratulated me on the new job in Hawaii. Closing that chapter on my teaching career in California was difficult. But, I was eager to open a new chapter with Hawaii.

Upon landing in Hawaii, I remember looking down over the chain of islands. While I was eager to start this new chapter, I was a bit nervous too. Uprooting your family and life as you know it can come with some reservations. It's the eagerness that pushes you beyond your fears especially when you are being called to do a greater work. I will admit that I didn't even tell my parents. I will never forget the shock and hurt on my mother's face. She couldn't believe I didn't tell her about this big move. I admit I was selfish. I didn't want the family to try and talk me out of this move. This was a major transition in my family's life. I tried to explain this to my mom. But, like any loving, caring mother, she wasn't buying one iota of it. I admit I was wrong, but my eagerness pushed me to step out on a limb and take the plunge. Once settling in and taking care of all the necessary paperwork to become an employee of Hawaii's Department of Education, life became real. Coming from the hustle and bustle of Los Angeles, to the laid back (take care of it when you can) Hawaii vibe, I was in heaven and mainly shock.

I was assigned to a beautiful campus located on a small island with majestic views of mountains and clear turquoise ocean. Let's say, monitoring recess was a step up from the sky ridden helicopters and police chases I experienced. But, I cherished every moment of it. Reality set in when I was assigned the worst caseload. My colleagues had gone through the same earlier. I guess it was my turn to work with the difficult students and their parents. Since I was the new teacher on the block, I was being thrown every difficult scenario. I fell into a state of depression in which I reached out to my mother. She said, "Oh no, you decided to make this decision behind our backs. You will need to stay right on that island and do what you signed up for!" I admit I had never lived away from my family. It was truly a wake-up call across the board. Here I was again, experiencing the teacher lounge mentality. I never did set foot in that teacher's lounge in Hawaii. I ate my lunch in my classroom while I worked on the endless paperwork.

In all my eagerness, I took on all those students, developed the curriculum and wrote students' Individualized Education Plans (IEPs). It was indeed a struggle! I remember asking the principal at the time if I could take a day off to write the IEP's. He responded with a stern, "No!" I had to suck it up and perform my job responsibilities just like the other special education teachers. At the time, I was upset and thought it to be a little unfair, but in the end, it taught me a valuable lesson. If you are purposed for this profession, you hold the responsibility to carry it out despite difficult times. Of course, I was still a newbie special education teacher, but my eagerness to tough it out paved my way. Thank you, mommy, for the tough love. And my family, who supported me during my downtimes. Plus, the principal who taught me not to give in when the going got tough. It is important to recognize those who are on your side even if they don't understand what you're experiencing.

As I have stated, teaching in Hawaii was the greatest time of my life. I not only developed my teaching skills, but I adopted an ohana (family). The faculty were close-knit and going to work felt like coming home. Faculty meetings became a potluck gathering. To this day, I remain close friends with my co-workers and my teaching assistants. Hawaii represented the true beauty of special education. The love and support felt for that population of students were heartfelt. I am positive there are other untapped places with the same amount of love and support. This was just my experience.

Will parents or families always be content with special education services? Of course not. But, the level of care and support I felt there was an undeniable sincere work of dedicated efforts. I truly felt the most laid back in delivering services which led to increasing my creativity. It was in Hawaii when I was encouraged to go back to college. This time, I eagerly enrolled in a Curriculum & Instruction Development Masters' program. Again, I worked full-time and attended classes at night for another grueling two years.

I developed a Preschool Early Intervention Curriculum for the state of Hawaii. I even directed and produced a public service announcement to promote the importance of Early Intervention for children with disabilities.

Eagerness has been the key to my success in this profession. I consider it to be another quality a special education teacher must possess. I am always eagerly looking for ways and strategies to improve my role as a special education teacher. The following strategy is how eagerness can contribute to a successful school year:

E - Entertain your thinking. I know this is easier said than done. We can read the best books with the best advice. It is a matter of following through on the advice. I was bombarded with strategies and methods to improve my teaching practice. I enjoyed the advice because it truly mimicked what I was experiencing on the campuses. I thank those teachers who took the time to impart people with their knowledge. But, what was missing was a book for special educators that truly approached the hard issues experienced on campuses. After teaching in four states, I saw a common theme: lack of support. In that case, one has to entertain ways at obtaining that support instead of complaining.

A - Accommodate your needs. We should know this strategy well. We do this for our students daily. But, fail to do it for ourselves as we are thrown in the trenches and expected to work our magic. Some might say, that it is a selfish strategy, but I respond with, "You are darn right it is!" If you are going to fight for the rights of your students, one must accommodate their approaches to ensure success. Not everyone is receptive to the plight of your students. Therefore, adopting accommodations for yourself to help stakeholders meet you halfway is a must.

G - Go-Getter mentality. If you're in this profession and you lack the drive to go after whatever it is you think will improve special education practices for your students, then I am going to quite frankly say, "Go-Get back your purpose!" One cannot lead in this profession without knowing what they are going after. At times, our attention can be focused on other things. But, you can make things happen one step at a time. You do not have to be complete all at once. Just go after whatever it is on your heart, and accomplish it.

E - Engage your audience. I am speaking of engagement from a different perspective. You need to hone in on your acting skills. Special education teachers wear many hats. You will have to learn to play many different roles.

R - Reasons are for seasons. There is a reason why ideas are emerging out of nowhere in your mind. You are being called to do something greater because of the season in your life. Don't lose these opportunities to act. Do not succumb to your fears or believe the time is not right. Still do it anyway. You never know whose life you are impacting.

Whether I am consistently researching resources, programs, studying different strategies, presenting at conferences, writing, or developing curriculum, I am eagerly researching for the next best thing to improve on special education practices. I like to stay ahead of the trends or at least stay knowledgeable of the trends. Many of my colleagues say, "You make teaching special education look effortless!" But, little do they know, they could be doing the same. Here's how.

Chapter 4: Effortlessly

It is often said that you ought to wake up each morning loving the work that you do. I know it sounds cliché, but it is a fair statement in my opinion. I will be honest; there are mornings when I do not want to get out of bed. I go through my morning rituals of getting ready just to beat traffic to get to work on time. However, once I am at work 45 to 60 minutes later, I am excited to be there. I know no other career would be this rewarding for me. This is the reason why work appears effortless to my colleagues. It is that "calling" I spoke of in Chapter 1 to purposively serve others with a passion.

I believe when you are operating in a spirit of selflessness, your work becomes effortless. You have been provided with the necessary tools to get the job done even if there is no more money in the budget to get the work done. It is not a magical process. It is a universal alignment that allows your efforts to match the needs of the students you are servicing. You were chosen for this position. You show up to work daily and perform exceedingly. Your desires are linked to your profession. Instead of complaining, you figure it out. It is no different than another individual being called to other professions and excelling. Doctors, attorneys and CEO's lead successful practices because of that very same calling. Colleagues are quick to say, "I don't know how you can do this every day, year after year? Don't you get tired?" I always respond, "It's a good thing you don't have to do this every day, year after year. And no, I don't grow tired of serving others."

It's that simple. Am I tired some days? Absolutely! I wouldn't be human if I didn't get tired. Work is work. The process of ensuring all facets of the job are being covered drains not only your mental capacity but also your physical capacity. One colleague who I adored once told me, "That's why work is called work. You don't just sit there, of course, you're going to be tired if you're working." You can still love and enjoy what you do, but be exhausted at the end of the day. It doesn't take away from your hard efforts. As special education teachers, it is important to take breaks and maintain a balance in your life.

Another colleague said, "You make working in special education look fun!" It's only fun because I enjoy what I do. The students I serve are phenomenal. Of course, there are tough days, but the good days outweigh those not-so-good days. It is easy to say now because I have matured in the profession. I have hit some hard walls. One does need to maintain a level of tactfulness. Colleagues, students, and parents will sometimes push you to your limits. Never succumb to their immature behavior by reacting to their actions. Remain tactful in all your dealings. These individuals may be going through some hard times. It's hard to remember this concept when dealing with individuals who lack regard for your feelings. This is when your special education teacher steps in to diffuse behaviors. We do it in our classrooms with our students. At times, adults can be babies including myself.

Individuals who appear to work effortlessly know the secret. It's about working smarter not harder. You utilize those around you to delegate tasks that help them to grow. I will share my following strategy with you to help you work effortlessly.

E - Enlist a team of quality individuals who are eager and not afraid to work. It is important to rally around people who share the same passion for making a difference. They live each day working on their purpose. It doesn't have to be a large team. Sometimes, a team of two can go a long way. Remember, you cannot do it alone. More can be accomplished with willing and able hands on deck.

F - Freedom from being tied down to work. Love what you do, and you will have a free mind while getting your work done. Others will judge you because it looks like you're not working. This is the beauty of being free from those negative mindsets. You were purposed for this position because you exercise the freedom to explore and expand.

F - Fair tactics are essential to working effortlessly. It is the notion of sharing the workload. It is the habit of delegating. It is only fair that all involved should carry out their roles. It isn't fair for one to share the entire load.

O - Open your mind to new ideas. This is how you grow as an individual. There is more than one way to complete a task. Other people have great ideas too, so embrace new ideas. Always remember the importance of collaboration.

R - Ready to move on things. It shouldn't take a lot of time to get the ball rolling. If your team decides on a project, then start acting on it. This is where many individuals get stuck in their own fear. Most people love the idea of sharing ideas, but very few acts on those ideas. The hemming and hawing on compliance monitoring begin to take effect. Stay ready to move things along.

T - Teach by example. The "know it all's" love to tell you how much they know because they have been there and done this and that. These are the same people who sit back, watch and do absolutely nothing to improve on special education skills. To the "know it all" people, stop acting like you are unable to learn new things. Teach rather than talk about people who are doing the work and taking the time to learn the profession. Teach people what you've acquired over the years, and also, be ready to learn.

L - Learn to get along with others. This strategy wins half the battle, even when you are at your wits ends. Close your mouth, think about why he or she is rattling your nerves and wish them the best in their endeavors. It is not worth it to engage in others' limited thinking or lack of character. This is a hard one for me as well. But I still exercise this strategy because it is a key step in achieving success.

E - Encourage yourself and others who are willing to make a difference. Negative thinking individuals bring people down. These individuals have underlying issues that you are not paid to counsel. Once you have shared your stance, move on to others who are ready to join your team.

S - Schedules help keep projects on task. Develop a habit of writing down timelines, due dates, and future project ideas. This habit will streamline your work load. Therefore, freeing up time handle other job tasks.

S - Strategize to combat potential threats to your day by thinking ahead. While we cannot avoid the impromptu, we can try to foresee the "what if's" by implementing back up plans. Do not allow yourself to become stressed out over situations outside of your control. I am still working on this strategy myself. It's a great strategy that ensures we are always ahead of our limitations.

L - Live life on purpose. Every day should be a day you work on something that drives your passion for serving others. This makes the school year go by fast, trust me. I love saying,

"Where did the time go?" at the end of a school year. A life lived on purpose is rewarding. It thrives on

Y - Your journey is what you make it. Take the time to write down what matters to you in your role as a special educator. We cannot avoid tough, long days, but we can choose how we address them.

Having taught for seven years in Hawaii, I was exposed to the beauty of special education on a beautiful island full of ALOHA. Networking and visiting other islands to observe other special education programs was an adventure. I learned a lot about the Hawaiian culture, its food, and history. During a difficult time of furloughs and the market bubbling, it was time to say "Aloha," to the island. Talk about a transition. I cried on Kailua beach with my best friend, my TA. She and I hiked all over the island. I remember the day we got lost on one of our many hikes. It was the day Michael Jackson died. If you ever get a chance to visit Hawaii or teach there, I wish you the best teaching experience. Take full advantage of what the island has to offer.

Once again, I was sent off with a big bang by my co-workers. Hawaiians go all out when they throw a party. I can remember the kind words and sentimental gifts imparted to each one of my coworkers as we laughed and cried during our goodbyes. I will never forget a special TA who drove everyone batty. She ended up being placed with me in my last school year. Again, my strategy for writing an IEP for her secretly allowed me to have a great working relationship with her. I was determined to build on her strengths and weaknesses.

She thanked me for treating her with respect, kindness, and patience. This TA had great ideas but not a good approach. She suffered from impulsiveness which led to many classroom interruptions. I found a meaningful task for her to keep her busy that she enjoyed. She used to be an accountant and missed working with numbers. Since I hate numbers and anything mathematically related, she landed the job of handling my grades and attendance. See, effortlessly at its' finest.

You still need to maintain a level of tactfulness in dealing with co-workers. This strategy was soon to be tested as I flew out of Honolulu International back over the chain of islands that I would greatly miss. A sad feeling came over me. Was I still passionate about teaching early childhood intervention? Next stop, Viva Las Vegas!!!

Chapter 5: Tactfulness

What happens in Vegas, stays in Vegas! Now that is tactfulness at its' finest. Las Vegas! Talk about a complete change in environment, physically and mentally. My cards were dealt with teaching in Las Vegas. I will never forget the phone call I received from the principal that scouted me out. A sweet voice on the other line had discovered my resume in their school system. She admitted that she had never done this before, but she felt the urge to call me. She saw that my experience was in early intervention and elementary. However, she liked the idea that I had a bachelor's in English. The principal asked if I would be interested in teaching English and Reading inclusion classes at the middle school level to students with disabilities. I did not want to come across as ungrateful for this opportunity. But, I had heard horror stories about middle school, so I was a little reluctant. I remained tactful in my responses because you never want to turn down an opportunity. My experiences had always been through a Human Resource representative. Although I felt a little intimidated by not having a middle school background, I did agree to an interview and a tour of the school.

This school was located right off the Las Vegas strip. Gone were the days of magical ocean views and cascading mountains in beautiful Hawaii. I was now staring at skyscraper hotels, sprawling tourists, and the towering Stratosphere's roof-top thrill rides. I was offered the position on the spot. I accepted and signed my contract the following day. Middle school was a set of its' own apples. It was in middle school where I learned to develop the strategy of tactfulness. Being new to the world of inclusion, I had a lot to learn about working with other colleagues. Gone were the days of having my students the entire day in one classroom and living in our bubble.

As an English/Reading inclusion teacher, I taught English and Reading resource/inclusion to 6th through 8th grade. I was all over that campus. I worked with an eclectic group of individuals in my department. The special education department was for lack of better words work in progress. At the end of my first year, I was offered the Department Chair position in special education. I was shocked, grateful and nervous at the same time. I knew my department would be up in arms. Here I was the new teacher on the block leading a team that was older than me and had years of middle school teaching experience.

My principal assured me that I had what it took to lead the department in a new direction. She also reassured me that she did not offer me the position because of my experience. Our special education department needed an overhaul. She admitted that it was for my tactfulness in dealing with my co-workers that earned me the position. She loved my ideas that I presented to her on improving our special education practices. There was a colleague of mine that lacked tactfulness. I co-taught Reading with her. This very sophisticated woman would say anything to get a rise out of anyone. I loved her dearly. She was a great teacher. However, she was growing tired of the classroom and couldn't retire. Her main agenda was to point out how everyone else wasn't doing their job. Before she died, her words of wisdom imparted still resonates, "Special education teachers need a swift kick to their backsides to get in line for these students!" All I could do was shake my head and heed her words of advice. She had a point. I'll forever remember her.

It can become frustrating when you work with negativity, constant complaining, and lack of innovation in finding solutions to fix issues. I picked up on this negative vibe the moment I stepped into the special department office on my initial tour of the school. But, I felt I was drawn to this school for a reason. Never in a million years had I imagined I would be a middle school teacher, not to mention the Department Chair. I spent the following year honing my leadership skills and learning to approach colleagues with the strategy of tactfulness.

As I think back on my earlier years of teaching and still to this day, I am mortified by the lack of tact on behalf of co-workers. If you are an individual who has ever experienced this lack of tact, I know how you feel. It makes you want to throw your hands up. It's a humiliating, embarrassing, and immature behavior especially when it is done in front of others (i.e., students). I want to apologize to anyone who has ever been put in this situation. It's downright rude. Those individuals need a wake-up call in learning the strategy of being tactful.

The art of being tactful takes consistent practice. I found this out when I taught my students how to use tact with one another during group work. I noticed that more positive conversations and collaborative efforts occurred to problem-solve issues. I strongly believe special education teachers who acquire the tactfulness quality will achieve success. I will break the tactfulness strategy down:

T - Take the time to hear what the other person is saying without interrupting. This automatically allows the individual to vent or share their perspectives without feeling intimidated or rushed. People need to remember the world does not solely revolve around their issues. Use this time to listen with intent.

A - Acknowledge the individual's perspective. This creates a sincere effort on your behalf that you are actively listening. This step develops a level of trust. It doesn't mean that you agree, but that you allowed these individuals the opportunity to express themselves.

C - Care in your response. Take the time to respond in a way that promotes a deeper level of understanding. Many people are quick to spout off what they think should happen because of their own experiences. News flash: we all have different dynamics affecting our reactions and interactions in similar situations. Care introduces a selfless approach to not make it about you, but about the situation. Your experiences do not negate others' experiences.

T - Table responses. Not every individual or situation calls for a response. By tabling responses, you allow time to process either the situation or the individual. This step gives you processing time to avoid negative exchanges. This is often practiced during IEP meetings. We all need a "cooling-off" period.

F - Feelings play a huge part in working with others. Some people are super sensitive while some lack sensitivity. Do not allow your feelings to cloud your judgment in responding to others. Often, our feelings can cause us to lash out or ignore others. This step reminds us of our purpose in serving others. We need to guard our feelings to make appropriate decisions.

U - Unique in our ways. This is the specialness that makes us. We are all different, yet united. Our paths have led us to be colleagues. The beauty of being unique is that we all have our unique talents and gifts to share. This step allows our uniqueness to bridge the gap in servicing others outside of ourselves.

L - Laugh, laugh and laugh more. Whether the situation is funny or serious, you should be able to laugh at something you or someone said, did, or didn't say or do. But you should try and understand the situation first before you laugh. Not all situations will accommodate laughter. This step is crucial in remaining true to who you are. It brings the joy and fulfillment to serve your purpose.

N - New you. Whether you are an experienced or a new teacher, maintain a newness about yourself. No one knows everything there is about the profession. Stop parading around like you are the expert just because you become specialized in an area. You too can be called on your profession and made to look foolish. This step allows one to be receptive to growing and learning in the profession. Yes, we are grateful to be surrounded by knowledgeable people, but maintain a humbleness about yourself.

E - Evolve with the trends. A part of addressing others in remaining tactful in exchanges is to know your stuff. You should be able to bring something to the table that supports your stance respectfully not aggressively. As educators, we should be looking for opportunities to evolve the profession and one another. There is nothing worse than conversing with an individual stuck in the old ways and days of handling issues within education. Continue the journey of learning, sharing, and evolving.

S - Stop pretending. It is perfectly okay not to know everything and remain professional. In fact, it is better to say that you do not know the answer than to stumble around words trying to appear knowledgeable. This is the step in which laughter can be infused. I am not encouraging making fun of others, but we all have a few of these individuals on our campuses.

S - Sanity remains balanced. Remember to avoid exchanges that cost you your sanity. We need to learn to pick our battles wisely. Not every situation is ours to battle. There is always that one co-worker who makes you feel like you are in the twilight zone. The ones who are professionals at creating their own circus. Please slowly back up and quickly walk the other way when you see them coming. You may not be cut out to handle that individual as well as Ms. King does. Let Ms. King use her tactfulness strategy to serve that individual a nice platter of reality.

There you have it! Tactfulness is a great strategy to practice in department meetings, team meetings or a workshop. This will make or break you in having a successful school year. Smiling and nodding only gets you far in life. Remember, you do have a voice, but learn to use it in a way that causes you to lead by example. I used to see teachers interrupt our school leaders during mid-speech in front of the faculty. One teacher was fired up and allowed her feelings to disrupt our faculty meeting. I found it to be rude and disrespectful. When you behave in this manner, you are behaving no better than the person you are calling out. This sends the wrong message. Adopting this strategy of tactfulness will help you improve on your journey of being a special education teacher.

After teaching in Las Vegas for 4 years, I was on another journey in special education. My experiences teaching and leading in Las Vegas presented challenges on some days, but not enough to steal my joy for the profession. I dealt with the best and worse in colleagues. I developed wonderful friendships with my students and life-long friendships with colleagues. It was another happy time in my career that will go down in the history books. I gained leadership skills that prepared me for my next destination. Next stop, Dallas Texas!

Chapter 6: Happy

Time to saddle that horse and cowgirl it up. Dallas, Texas here I come. The journey of moving to Texas was presented with an opportunity to lead again in a special education department. I attended a job fair in which I met an angel who scouted me out in passing. She asked me for my resume and said that her principal was going to love me. As I was leaving the job fair, I saw her running down the aisle toward me, waving me down, shouting, "Sweetheart, my principal wants to meet you right now!" She grabbed my arm, and we were both clicking and clacking in our heels toward the school's hiring table. This lady, who I called my guardian angel was vibrant and full of true Texan "Yee-Haw" pride.

I have had several angels within my career guiding me throughout this profession. But she was super special in so many ways. I never heard the word "Boo" used so much in my life. I loved her happy spirit and Texas twang. Her favorite phrase, "I got you, Boo!" After meeting with the principal and learning she and I shared similar experiences, I was instantly hired. Again, I met another principal who afforded me another opportunity to grow in my leadership and teaching skills.

As a young child, I grew up in Texas on an Air Force base. My mom jokes to this day, "You never stopped until you got back there!" I gave my parents a hard time. I was that child that left kicking and screaming during military relocations. But, here I was back in the country of Texas. I was super happy. I would be teaching in another school that was nestled in the hood. This high school introduced new dynamics that stretched me beyond my comfort zone.

This was going to be another teachable moment in my career. I loved the campus. The neighborhood was charming; it was even considered the hood. I was happy to be teaching again in that type of environment. The sea green waters of relaxation and bright lights of the strip were faint memories. Coming back to reality and touching the lives of inner-city students with disabilities was back on my agenda. I genuinely loved my students and colleagues. But I did encounter pushback from some co-workers. Again, that goes with the territory. Being the new teacher on the block can cause intimidation, hostility, and threats to positions. It was all meant to grow me.

Teaching at the high school level was almost like dealing with colleagues who never grew up from high school. The drama and backstabbing among the staff were equal to those of the students. But who was I to judge? I engaged in it as well. I became sucked into the cliques that formed and without realizing it, we were turning into bullies against one another. Without going into any specifics, I was still happy to be there. I was learning how to develop a growth mindset of dealing with colleagues professionally and from a distance. I was chosen to serve on a Leadership Team with my administrators that opened my eyes to the reality of people's journeys and why they behave the way they do. We spent a lot of time outside of school including Saturdays growing our knowledge on establishing foundations that build successful teams to increase academic success for our students.

I learned a lot about working together during times when I didn't feel like it. But, that was the purpose. We ask this of our students with disabilities and expect them to get along with others' when they don't feel like it either. I grew up personally and professionally teaching at the high school level. I learned to meet people where they are even if I did not personally understand it. I started to impart this strategy of remaining "Happy" to my students because without fail they brought that same drama into the classroom. As a matter of fact, the popular song at that time was Happy by Pharrell. This song became the theme song during my two-year stint at the high school level. Believe it or not, the art of being happy is a quality that carries over to your students and their success. I had to find a strategy that related to my students' experiences to redirect their behavior and invite happiness back into the classroom. I implemented the following strategy in my classroom.

H - Haters will always be there. You must understand not everyone is going to like you. Haters deserve a little credit. They fuel your fire. They motivate you to keep being the best that only you know how to be. Haters are your secret fans. They are secret faithful followers who took it upon themselves to watch over you and ignore themselves. They don't realize it because they are too busy investing time in what you are doing instead of improving themselves.

A - Acceptance of yourself. Do not depend on others' acceptance of you. True acceptance comes from within. I will rather be happy within than beg from another person's warped sense of acceptance. You spend the most time with yourself. Your acceptance of yourself is the priority. A priority that leads you to your true independence.

P - Positivity goes further. Maintain positive thoughts about your situations and your future. Do not let anyone steal your joy. If people have an issue with your positivity, they have the option not to deal with you. Like you have the option to avoid their negativity.

P - Playful is the key to maintaining happiness. Share funny stories, laugh at jokes, play music, dance, and allow moments to be silly. Have fun and laugh at yourself. Enjoy being put on blast as my students often say. It makes you transparent and human.

Y - You can only be who you are. Live your life as if every day depends on you to make a difference. Only you can make the changes that you see are needed within. Love you!

Ask anyone I have ever worked with closely about my stance on remaining happy. Even though we go through rough patches in our profession, personal lives and with one another; I refuse to let anyone steal my happiness. I believe if I am given the power and authority to control something, my happiness will be first on my list. Our students are looking to us to model this. I am reminded of a student who is obsessed with movie characters. This student would carry a doll version of a movie character with us on community trips. This toy doll represented the happiness he wanted to feel. Life-imitating art. Others stared awkwardly; I didn't find it to be weird. I admired this student's quiet strength to be different, but still happily stand out. To be effective, your ability to remain happy allows students with disabilities to understand that despite their setbacks, they can still enjoy their lives. As I watched my seniors mature and graduate into a world that sometimes lacks empathy, I know the strategies taught in our class discussions will carry them a long way. Make me proud, guys!

On the last day of school, I laid my head on my desk, stared down at my knee-high boots, and knew in my heart I needed a change. Teaching at the high school level for two-years was a wake-up call. There was more I needed to be doing for our students with disabilities graduating from our high schools. My guardian angel imparted her words of wisdom, "Sweetheart, those boots are made for walking. You're not bound to this campus! Go touch other students' lives!" That year, not only did I take her advice, she did too. She spread her wings and departed from this earth. Now, she is looking down on me making sure I am the sweetheart she helped to groom. I did spread my wings and sped (no pun intended) to a different school district within Texas. Gone were my high school days, so I thought.

Chapter 7: Empathetic

The beauty of special education is the different paths it can lead you on. If you are called to this profession, you should never have to succumb to burn out or boredom. Just when you start to feel the burn or lack of excitement, appears an opportunity to easily change lanes and explore a different area. I knew I was done with high school. I had learned the hard lessons that I needed to learn. I was grateful because I made amazing connections with people and families. That summer, I knew something had to give. I didn't know how, when, or where, but I knew a change was coming.

I received a phone call for an interview from a different school district. I thought I was going to interview for a position that I originally applied for. Once in the interview, I was told there wasn't a position. I thought that this was a sick joke. Why would they invite me to an interview if there wasn't a position?

The employer read through my resume and nodded with each bullet point. She felt that I had the qualifications to develop an 18+ transition program for the school district. They thought I would be the best person for the job and offered me a contract. I am still picking my mouth off the floor from that interview. This was happening! My employer ended up becoming an amazing leader to work for. Her passion, drive, and motivation to see me do great things fueled my purpose. She believed in my abilities. Isn't that what we all want? She gave me back what I knew I had all along but hidden within me, empathy. I was back to my writing and developing curriculum.

I knew it was time to create a transition program in which students with disabilities are exposed to job training, volunteerism, and post-secondary educational opportunities. This population of students is told throughout their school life they can become employed and attend college. Unfortunately, not everyone believes this about our students. The empathy that is lacking in the world of employment is due to the lack of awareness not necessarily ignorance. While people can be ignorant, I feel ignorance is only a result of people choosing not to accept our students after learning of their capabilities. Shame on those people. I remain tactful and remind them that you never know who you will have to rely on to help you. It's information to grow on to increase empathy.

We are living in the 21st century, and this capacity to impart empathy has still yet to be reached. As special educators, our role is to continue to help others understand the capabilities of our students. Here is the following strategy I developed for approaching and introducing my students to the community and increasing empathy:

E - Educate yourself and others. Only you know and feel what you allow yourself to experience. Whether you are doing your research on a disability or learning from the students, parents or their teachers, stay educated. This step helps with understanding students with disabilities and their capabilities.

M - Motivate yourself and others to see the purpose in students with disabilities' lives. They too have dreams and aspirations. While we must maintain realistic expectations, motivation allows these students to work towards their passions instead of sitting at home on the couch or playing video games all day after they graduate. Motivating these students is essential as with any one of us.

P - Provide experiences and opportunities to assist students with disabilities in your businesses or those you can recommend people to, on college campuses, or organizations. These students are told throughout their schooling that these are readily available resources to them. Only to be turned away because people pass judgment on their abilities.

A - Allow them to explore and find out what they can do in your establishments. You would be surprised at what these students can accomplish.

T - Think about how you would feel if this was you or a family member. How would you want to be treated? How would you respond to this kind treatment? This is a simple step, but you would be surprised by the thoughts that impede our judgment. Just be mindful.

H - Help where you see a need. If you see a student with a disability struggling, find out what you can do to help. Help comes in different packages (i.e., support, funding, resources). You will be amazed by the resources available to improve on special education programs that go untapped.

Y - Yield for these students what is rightfully theirs. Everyone deserves a chance. Always work on providing a platform for them to thrive on their abilities. Also, take time out to learn for yourself.

Anyone who has been called to special education has the empathy instinct. It goes along the territory of thinking outside of yourself. I am not seeking others to feel sorry for our students. Indeed, we all have limitations; however, understanding where an individual is mentally and developmentally can make the difference in how we see that individual through their situations.

Currently, I am still working in transition. I love it. In fact, it is rewarding to see students at this end of the spectrum. I plan on working in this area of special education for a while because there is a high need to ensure our students are graduating with opportunities. As you are probably learning by now, I have made some major transitions throughout my role as a special educator. I am happy to report that I am now a proud permanent resident of Texas.

As I have shared, special education covers a wide spectrum of services. In my many years of service in special education, I have met amazing individuals. You never know when bridges may be crossed on your journey. I was recently contacted by an old colleague. She is now the director of the Education Department at a private university. We worked together at my first school in Los Angeles, California. She and I braved the teacher's lounge together at times. Not to deviate from my point, this colleague offered me an adjunct professor position for her special education program. I couldn't thank her enough for this opportunity. I am now giving back the gift of special education to new special education teachers stepping up to the plate for our students.

Chapter 8: Adaptable

In any career field, learning how to be adaptable is the secret sauce. This goes hand in hand with being flexible, understanding, and patient. As we know, the landscape of special education will continue to expand. I believe this area of adaptability is most felt with our experienced teachers. New teachers are starting to learn this concept during their teacher programs. Anyone entering special education should be preparing themselves to relax, take a deep breath, listen and learn as you go. I can't begin to tell you the number of teachers I have encountered that never know when to stop talking. They need to say something because they are trying to prove their knowledge to others. They are like that one student in your class who fails to raise their hand and shouts out the answers. No matter how many times you tell little Johnny how inappropriate it is, he doesn't see the need to stop.

Please do not be that special education teacher. I am not trying to silence you or take away your freedom of speech.

Do not misinterpret this point. I am simply saying there are times and places for venting your frustrations or proving your knowledge. Next time, you feel the urge to act out on your impulses, pretend you are the teacher in your class. Would you expect that behavior from any of your students?

The best special education teacher is the one who models adaptability. This is an important concept to also drive home in your classrooms with your students. On a daily, I write the agenda on the smartboard. I also prepare my students for interruptions to that agenda. Our students need to learn how to adapt when things do not work out as planned. It is a hard lesson for our students, especially with our autism population of students. But, guarantee, they understand the concept after it has occurred repeatedly.

We need to teach our students with disabilities Real-Ville curriculum. Gone are the days of sugarcoating our curriculum. These students need a dose of reality. There is a real world waiting out there to swallow them whole. My current teaching position affords me the creative space to teach adaptability. Co-workers ask me what curriculum am I using. I quickly reply, "the community is our curriculum." Everything our students need to learn is right outside our job center's door. Colleagues are quick to minimize transition programs as a year of spending days going on field trips. Again, that is the beauty of teaching in transition. Our students are receiving real-life experiences that can be generalized from the classroom to the community. Transition programs vary in their approaches to learning. Not all transition programs will look the same. They should be based on the students' individual needs. Here's another strategy for teaching being adaptable:

A - Adventurous spirit. Seek adventure in everything that you do. Although, there will be times that change comes when you least likely expect it. Find the adventure in making it a new challenge for yourself and your students.

D - Dedicate to your purpose. Remember the reason that you are in your current position. You signed up to be a special educator for students with disabilities. These students need you to keep it together. Dedication says a lot about the teacher who spent the entire night before writing lesson plans only to hear from an administrator, "These are written incorrectly!" The teacher takes those lessons, revamps them despite the inclination to vent her frustrations to the administrator. And she nails her lessons from here on out.

A - Available in the good and bad times. Every day will not be perfect. Avail yourself to situations outside of your control. This process grows your resilience. Your students are watching you.

P - Participate in ways that make a difference. You can practice this step by simply starting clubs on campuses that meet your student's interests and needs. Find opportunities to keep your students active. Explore opportunities within the community. I laugh when colleagues minimize my transition program to field trips. I do not know one student who has not enjoyed or benefitted from being out in the community exploring and learning. Wake up people; learning does not just occur in classrooms. Every community trip our students take is provided with a lesson plan. Yes, they do have fun and enjoy themselves, so what?

T - Trust yourself. We know that we can't control every situation. But, knowing you can trust yourself to do the right thing for your students is half the battle. It can be difficult to trust other colleagues who may have ulterior motives and seek to sabotage. If your heart is in the right place, trust yourself to be adaptable.

A - Acknowledge the situation for what it is. This is an important process in dealing with co-workers. You can't change how other people behave or react. But, you can acknowledge there's something off about them and continue to focus on what's important. Remember haters are truly your friends.

B - Believe in the process. Just like our students, we as special educators are growing and maturing in the profession. Believe you were chosen for this profession because you have a gift to offer to your students. Do not allow colleagues, students or parents to rob you of your journey.

L - Learn from everyone. Remember you're not the only teacher on the campus. As situations arise, pay close attention to how others' respond. Our students are our best teachers too. You must have the ability to accept that situations arise as "teachable moments."

E - Ego aside. I can't stress this enough. Special education is multifaceted. While one person may be knowledgeable in one area, it doesn't make them the expert across the board. We should be here to support one another. I am learning not to allow others' opinions influence how I teach. Every teacher is different in how they impact their students' lives.

I would have to say that this step has been my favorite throughout my career. Most of my colleagues would probably say that sometimes I am too laid back. Personally, I do not see the need to be up in arms over everything. Again, learning how to pick your battles will carry you further in this field. I have worked with colleagues who have Obsessive Compulsive Disorder (OCD) and Know It Allness (KIA). Believe it or not, I have learned a lot from them too. I learned what I do not want to be like. I do not feel the need to stress over everything due to fear of being out of compliance or being ridiculed.

As ethical special educators, we all know the right thing to do. Stop the habit of comparing each other. We all have our unique style that we bring into our classrooms. We need to maintain a realistic approach to our situations. This is the beauty of special education. You can choose your area of expertise. Grow and mature in that area. Then teach others how to be successful in that area. As special educators, we have our reasons for signing our contracts and showing up every day. Maintaining a realistic approach to carrying out

your job responsibilities is another strategy that has helped
me over the years.

Chapter 9: Realistic

Everyone likes to think special educators are miracle workers. Believing we have the magical ability to cure students with disabilities and solve every problem. As much as I want to be able to possess that power, it's not realistic. This is another grey area within special education. Many of our colleagues and parents will expect us to perform miracles. Part of the battle in working in special education is to understand the tough realities that will arise from certain situations. There needs to be a system in place for realistic goals in approaching every situation.

Even as a transition teacher, I must be aware of realistic goals and objectives I create for my adult students. I have administrators or colleagues question me whether I thought a goal that I set for a student was realistic. I hate those type of questions. It can sometimes leave you second-guessing yourself. This is where special education can become tricky. The dynamics that play into each student within your classroom that others do not see can become unnerving.

People are quick to tell you what you're doing wrong and question your activities. This is when reminding them respectfully that you are the special education teacher and you know realistically what the student is capable of underneath your direction. In a perfect world, other colleagues would be supportive of one another. Unfortunately, this is the reality we are all encountering on our campuses. This is a strategy I created in dealing with colleagues, students, and parents that I implement year after year:

R - Ready or not; it's happening. As stakeholders, we must address upcoming transitions. Whether we are prepared for it or not. We need to remain mindful of issues that need to be addressed before we make decisions. It's not enough to talk about upcoming changes. We need to be ready to address them.

E - Entertain ideas and choose what appropriately fits the situation. Allow yourself the opportunity to gather ideas and resources consistently. It is important to have a bank of resources to choose from. This will allow the team to discuss different options in which the team can choose which is best for the student.

A - Advocate for yourself and your students. We tell parents that they are their own child's best advocate. While this is true, so should we be for our students and ourselves. As special educators, we want the best for our students. We need to start acting like it.

L - Legalities are a constant. This is the necessary red tape all of us succumb to. However, stay knowledgeable of the laws and find opportunities that do not affect compliance issues. Of course, this is a team effort. But do not allow legalities to take hold of your creativity to grow special education practices.

I - Independently think for yourself. Do not allow other's sometimes limited view, knowledge or position impede how you feel about your capabilities. Do not get lost in the sea of special education teachers who depend on others to tell them what to do. We are all different in our thinking. I do value others' input, but I can't allow others' negative thinking cloud my judgment.

S - Situations change. You will not always make the right decisions at the right time and you may. Just understand there are some things outside of our control. Do not beat yourself up over it. This is one of the areas where being adaptable is highly effective.

T - Truthfulness is key in this process. Sometimes colleagues, students, and families need to hear the truth about their student and what they are capable of. We need to get comfortable with having those tough conversations. Try to put yourselves in their shoes. The truth goes much further.

I - Inquire into opportunities that extend outside of the school realm. Research grant opportunities to help support colleagues, students, and families which you're not able to offer with school resources.

C - Caution is always wise. Of course, we never rush into things without doing our due diligence. Do not confuse this point with being fearful. This step exercises judgment in ensuring the success of being realistic in situations and improving the success of our students.

Special education teachers are human. We are not magicians. However, we can use these strategies to make magic happen by working together. Maintaining a realistic perspective and doing the best that we can do in every situation is the best miracle anyone can produce in helping our students with disabilities succeed.

As we are nearing the end of our journey, I have shared strategies that have been influential throughout my special education journey. These strategies were learned over time and in time. Everyone's journey will be different. We all are experiencing the ups and downs of special education. But, I would like to impart one more strategy that is crucial to this whole process. This is the art of timeliness. Now, this will be the link that bounds the chain to your success in special education. Shall we proceed? Let's go.

Chapter 10: Timely

If you have made it to this part of the book, Congratulations! You made it in time. You are on your way to a successful journey in special education, timeliness. Remember, we live in a world ruled by numbers that stare back at us through clocks, cell phones, and computers. Everyone's time is valuable, and they will let you know it. We do need to be mindful of this. Our time is just as equally important. Schools across the world have depended on time since educations' inception. The importance of remaining timely covers a gamete of areas within special education. Having your paperwork in order and an organizational system is highly important. I have been dinged many times for being insensitive to others' time even if I had the best intentions. It's just one of the tricks to the trade you figure out as you go. What I consider valuable, others may not, so you become a good reader of facial cues and swift kicks underneath the table. These things really do happen. But, it doesn't have to happen to you. I am from the school of thought of learning by trial and error. I've made my mistakes. I now know how to circumvent them. If you are new or an experienced special education teacher and still making these mistakes, I want to share my strategy for remaining timely.

T - Timing practice. That's right, practice your timing. I know that it is not ideal for most situations. Others too can affect your timing. I would chart out my timing to cover important topics that I have identified as needs to be addressed. Allow others' time to speak. Timing also affects paperwork. Allow yourself enough time to write your IEP's and file your paperwork.

I - Intentional information. Meetings are scheduled for a purpose. Be clear in your intentions. Review your agenda and communicate that the goal is to stick to the allotted time of the meeting. Meetings can be sidetracked with stories and background information. This is fine if it is relevant to the topic. Do not let too much time lapse on information that can be expounded on after the meeting.

M - Message should be clear. Whoever you're dealing with, be forthcoming. These are opportunities for you to address issues that somebody may need to hear at that time. Keeping messages clear and concise helps you address issues faster while dealing with others. This, in turn, saves you time.

E - Equal timing. Allow everyone to have an equal chance to share their perspective. Stop interrupting others while sharing their opinions. Write down any thoughts you may have. You can address those after the meeting.

L - Long-winded conversations need to be curtailed. People who are long-winded will repeat their story countless times by adding a different spin. Even if you have told them you heard the same story before, they do not care. These people like to hear themselves talk. Try to avoid these people if you can, especially if you are working. They steal your time and attention away from your purpose.

Y - Years have gone by. If you start to feel like your exchange or meeting will never end. Take reign over the situation. We do not have an entire year to listen to the same issues. Do something about it.

The importance of timeliness is a serious setback for many special education teachers. Start writing down your upcoming IEPs and working on them in advance. It will save you time and stress in the end. There is no feeling like sitting in an IEP meeting and still trying to write sections. It looks unprofessional, and it is disrespectful to the others in the meeting. I understand some times call for one to be on a computer during a meeting. However, one needs to monitor their time on it. A colleague of mine used to work on her computer during our meetings. Parents were infuriated. They had every right to feel that way. During an important conversation, all we could hear were fingertips clicking. Be mindful of your behaviors in a meeting. People are watching for your attention.

Although no one likes to be judged, the fact remains we are being judged regardless. As special education teachers, we are purposed to be sincere in all efforts for our students. The strategies shared from my experience have worked not only for me but for my students and colleagues. As I have shared, no one knows all there is to know about special education. We may share similar experiences, but we do need one another's support. It is a challenging area of education, but I feel we can all learn from one another. I can't speak for others, but this book is timely.

Conclusion

Since its' inception, special education teachers have been key to the heralding efforts of providing and ensuring a Free Appropriate Education (FAPE) in classrooms across the world. From adhering to the required courses to obtaining specialized teaching degrees to the ongoing training and the array of disabilities they are faced with, special education teachers continue to be an asset to the field of education. As the transformation of special education continues to evolve with initiatives like No Child Left Behind Act (2002) and reauthorizations to special education laws, Individuals with Disability Education Act (IDEA, 2004) trickling down into classrooms, so are the evolving numbers of special education teachers leaving their students behind. If you google special education blogs, you will find these disturbing statistics that can no longer go unnoticed.

All of us are sweethearts of special education in our unique way. We hold the hearts of our students' year after year. Like a box of sweetheart candy, you never know which message you will be sent or given. It is important to think outside of the box. Treat every school year with a clean slate. Try not to harbor ill feelings or resentment toward colleagues or school leaders. This behavior will indicate what type of school year you will have. Remain positive and proactive throughout the school year. We do not learn from a bitter heart. Stay sweet in your dealings. Believe it or not, your students are taking note of your character as well as your colleagues.

Take each school year a day at a time. You will find each day has a built-in lesson that is preparing you to grow in the profession. Whether you are old or new in the profession, you are making an impact in the lives of students with disabilities.

We are a part of the history-making process. Let's continue to show up for our students with courage, determination, and purpose. It has truly been an honor and pleasure sharing not only my journey but the strategies that have worked throughout my career. We need to continue supporting each other by sharing our tricks to the trade across the world. Will you be that special education teacher that supports the downtrodden colleague? We need to be consistently reminded of the positive work that we do. Don't be afraid to make major moves that improve the state of special education on your campuses. You never know how your positive impact can affect other campuses across the world.

We have special gifts that need to be unwrapped on our campuses. Will you unwrap yours?

One important takeaway, you are not bound to just your campuses. Be bold and seek out opportunities to grow yourself in this profession. Now is the time to begin new trends that shape the way we provide special education. Best of luck to all of you and your endeavors to improve the state of special education.

Extension Exercises

Take some time to reflect on your sincere efforts. Write down the characteristics that represent your sincere efforts in working in special education.

Reflect on your willingness in your role as a stakeholder to improve practices, policies or reforms in special education.

List some ways in which you represent eagerness to be instrumental in leading change in special education.

In what ways do you lead effortlessly in your role as a special education stakeholder?

Not everyone is born with the tactful ability. In what areas do you need to work on in remaining tactful?

Remaining happy is a choice. How will you choose to maintain your happiness throughout a difficult school year?

As we expect others to have empathy for our situations, how will you express empathetic practices?

Learning to be adaptable to changing situations can be difficult. How will you address remaining adaptable while remaining true to your purpose?

Write down realistic goals for yourself for the school year?

Identify 5 areas in which you can exercise timeliness.

www.ingramcontent.com/pod-product-compliance
Lightning Source LLC
Chambersburg PA
CBHW071420040426
42445CB00012BA/1231